Bear Hugs

By KATHLEEN HAGUE
Illustrated by MICHAEL HAGUE

Henry Holt and Company
New York

Published by Henry Holt and Company, Inc., 115 West 18th Street, New York, New York 10011.
Published in Canada by Fitzhenry & Whiteside Limited, 195 Allstate Parkway, Markham, Ontario L3R 4T8.

Library of Congress Cataloging in Publication Data

Hague, Kathleen.
Bear hugs / by Kathleen Hague : illustrated by Michael Hague. — 1st ed.
p. cm.
Summary: A collection of poems about teddy bears and the things they do,
such as provide comfort at bedtime and engage in a game of hide-and-seek.
ISBN 0-8050-0512-9
1. Teddy bears—Juvenile poetry.   2. Children's poetry, American.
[1. Teddy bears—Poetry.   2. American poetry.]   I. Hague, Michael, ill.   II. Title.
PS3558.A32344B44   1989   811'.54—dc19   88-28458

Henry Holt books are available at special discounts
for bulk purchases for sales promotions, premiums,
fund-raising, or educational use. Special editions
or book excerpts can also be created to specification.
For details, contact: Special Sales Director, Henry Holt & Co., Inc.,
115 West 18th Street, New York, New York 10011.

First edition
Designed by Marc Cheshire
Printed in the United States of America
1 3 5 7 9 10 8 6 4 2

Hugs to
Juniper
Gabriel
Austin
Graham
Meghan
Brittany
Devon
John
Shannon
Ryan
Tim
Anthony

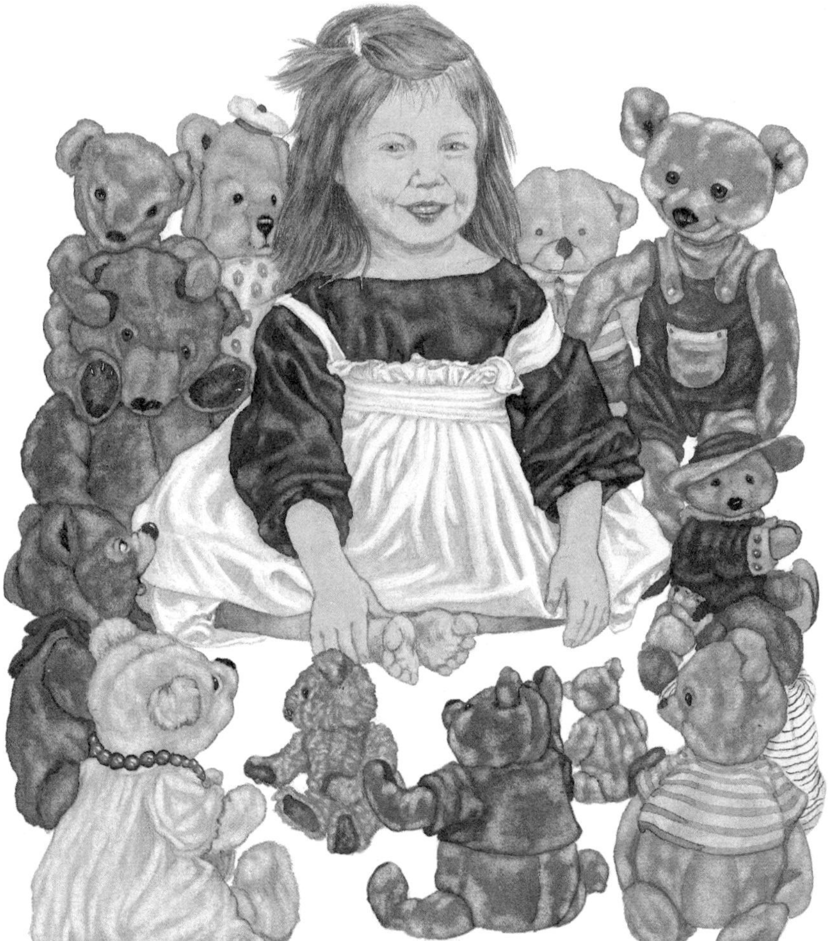

Teddy Bears

I like to talk to teddy bears;
They always have the time
To listen till I'm really through
With stories that are mine.

They never interrupt me
To ask when? why? or who?
And I think it's grand that they
Can keep a secret, too.

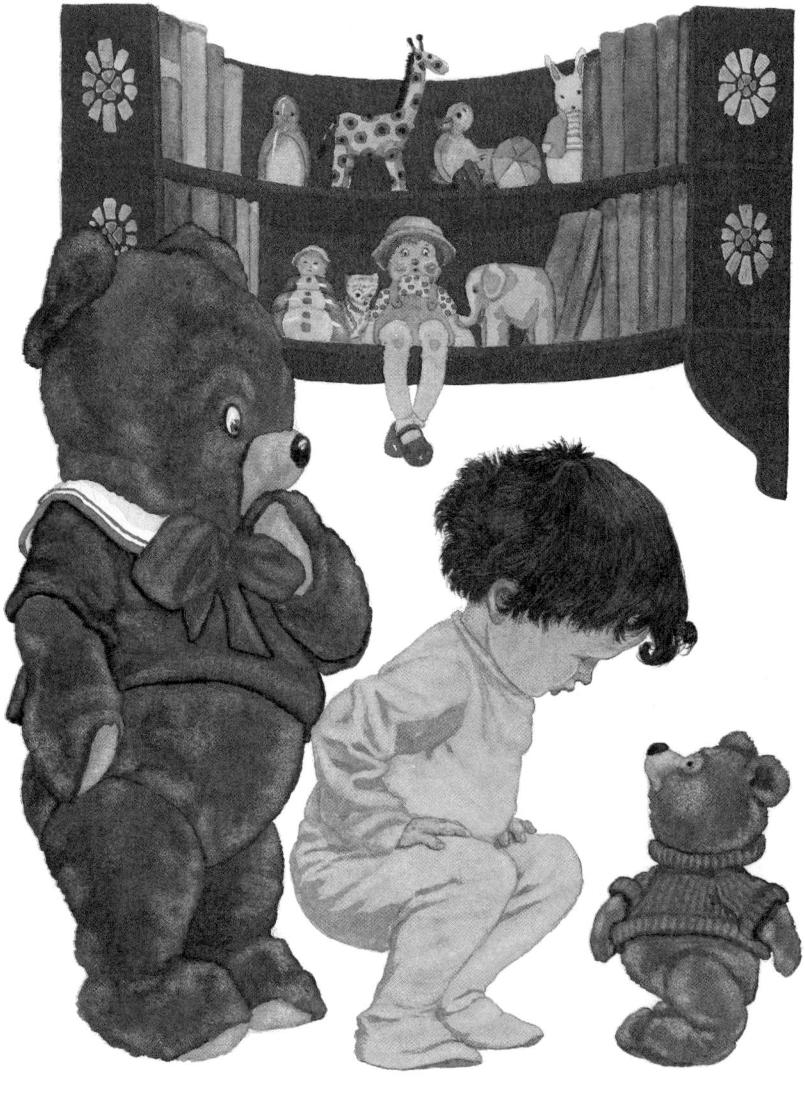

Me in the Middle

Big bear,
small bear,
me
in
the
middle.
Even though
there's
three
of
us,
together
we're
still
little.

Bedtime

When it's time to go to bed,
I do not mind.
I go instead
And climb the steps
That are the stair—
Up we go, just me and bear.

In the bed beneath the down
I snuggle warm.
It's hard to frown
In such a place,
And so we grin—
Bear at me and me at him.

Evening shadows glide and fall
Across the floor
And up the wall.
We haven't time
To count our sheep—
Bear and I are fast asleep.

Old Bear

Made of cloth instead of skin,
Only cotton stuffed within,
Cross-stitched eyes, an odd-shaped nose,
A tatted smile that seems to grow.

Here We Go, There We Go

Here we go,
There we go.
Right into bed we go,
Sleepy-eyed teddy and me.

Here we go,
There we go.
Never mind which way we go,
The wind is fair on the sea.

Here we go,
There we go.
Never mind where we go,
The dream world is ours to see.

Here we go,
There we go.
Never mind how fast we go,
The speed is go-as-you-please.

Here we go,
There we go.
Never mind when we go,
It's back in the morning with me.

Here we go,
There we go.
Back into bed we go,
Home from the lullaby sea.

Hairy Jones

Hairy Jones, Brittany's bear,
Was furry to the touch.
His eyes are gone.
His tummy's wrong.
He's been hugged and loved so much.

Hide-and-Seek

Eleanor lost her teddy bear.
She thought he'd run away.
She tried to find him everywhere
And called, "Please come and play."

She begged her mother, "Come and help."
"Of course I will," Mom said.
They found him playing hide-and-seek
Underneath her bed.

My Friend

My teddy bear is soft and brown.
His heart is warm and good.
No matter if I laugh or frown,
I know I'm understood.

Bear Hugs

It's the hug that wraps around you.
Its meaning is clear from the start.
There's no mistaking a real bear hug.
It's the one that's straight from the heart.